TAKE NOTHING

Books by Deborah Pope

Falling Out of the Sky
Fanatic Heart
Mortal World

TAKE NOTHING

DEBORAH POPE

Carnegie Mellon University Press
Pittsburgh 2020

Acknowledgments

Thank you to the editors of the following journals in which some of these poems first appeared:

Atlanta Review: "Encounter," "Gold Triumph Tulips"
Birmingham Poetry Review: "To the Next to Last Howard Johnson's,"
    "Visiting Hours with My Grandmother"
Cave Wall: "Voyage Out," "White Cyclamens"
The Cortland Review: "Late August"
Epoch: "The Dream of Eadfrith"
Michigan Quarterly: "Once in Canterbury Cathedral"
Poetry East: "Finding My Father"
Poetry Northwest: "In the Poetry Workshop"
Southern Humanities Review: "At the Other End of the Line"
Southwest Review: "Mother's Great-Aunt Irene" [published as "Irene"]
Tar River Poetry: "On Old State Route 10," "Threshold"
Tor House Journal: "Take Nothing" (recipient of the 2018 Robinson
    Jeffers Award), "Waiting for the Perseid Meteor Shower"

"The Healer" appeared in *Intimacy: An Anthology*: Jacar Press, ed. Richard Krawiec.

Cover art by Marianne Thompson, www.mariannethompson.com, thmare@gmail.com

Book design by Juliana Schnerr

Library of Congress Control Number 2019953778
ISBN 978-0-88748-656-2

10   9   8   7   6   5   4   3   2   1

for Dean

Contents

III

I

Threshold

Every beginning
is a detour.

Every choice bears the seed
of another.

A fool's errand is not
always foolish.

All systems tend to dismay.

If one door closes and another opens,
be wary in the passage between.

If truth is fire, you may shout it
in a crowded theater.

Nostalgia means to return home
and survive.

To forgive is to draw
to an inside straight.

Enlightenment is the child
of astonishment.

Unhappiness is the child
of postponement.

If a sage says, *Sell your cleverness
and buy bewilderment*, do it.

If a stranger says,
I have a story to tell you,
listen.

To the Next to Last Howard Johnson's

*One of only two Howard Johnson's left is closing
its doors in Bangor, Maine, due to lack of business.*
—News item

Goodbye, Howard of the orange roofs,
the turquoise spires, the fried clams,
hamburgers and milkshakes in 24 flavors.
Goodbye, Johnson of the aqua pools
we begged for on the long, hot cross-country
drive out west in a Chevrolet with a room
air conditioner bolted on a frame
to the driver's side window, freezing
my father, while the other cranked up
windows sweated the bejeezus
out of three kids pinching for space
in the back. Goodbye, car of a father
who said, "bejeezus," "how 'bout them apples,"
and how high 60 cents was for gas
at some last chance Esso, Pure or Sinclair.
Car of smoke, ashtrays and a steering knob
on a wheel big as a tire. Goodbye,
Stuckey's and Mail Pouch, walk-up
Dairy Queen huts with coiled turbans
of vanilla, cracking chocolate,
and perspiring mugs of A&Ws on sticky,
vinyl seats. Goodbye, heat mirages
on rolling two-lane roads, restroom keys
on wooden rectangles by greasy car lifts,
keys that led around to peeling doors
opening on doll-size basins and crickets.
Goodbye to counted states on single color
license plates, one-story brick motels,
teepees and cabins in a circle.
Oh newspaper-sized maps taking us
to the promised land of Penny and Sky King,
Pa and Johnny McCain, black-brimmed
Paladin, that we watched on our black-and-white

Crosley with Sunday night pizza on TV trays,
listening for "Maverick, ring your bell,"
all of us together.
You know, together.

On the Lake of Two Rivers, Ontario

I was already awake when my father nudged me
before dawn, had slept dressed for this.
I was proud of doing things other girls didn't—
build fires, trim kerosene lanterns, coolly
bait a hook and string a fish.

Loading the tackle, we shoved off on the immense,
mist-heavy water, leaving behind the murderous
black flies, food slung in the trees away from bears,
our pine-circled campsite with the old, pop-top
Nimrod trailer, the rest of the family asleep.

My father eased into his strokes,
the low blades skimming and dimpling the water.
In a while, sensing a position, he shipped the oars
and we lifted red worms and night crawlers
from their cardboard boxes like Chinese takeout.
Then readying our rods, we settled in,
the light just beginning to pale.

I'd like to say in the time that passed
we talked of deeper things, that my father
passed on to me some experience or wisdom
I never forgot. But we were fishing.
We would have been quiet, enclosed
in a companionable, understood *being*,
a meaning better than talk.

When we finally headed back, a line of perch
and bass trailed alongside the boat.
Pulling it back on land, breathing the tang
of the conifers, it seemed barely morning yet.
No one else was up, not even my brother,
whom he might have chosen instead.

Landscape with Figures

She stands on a platform in a lake,
squinting at the sun. Noon pours
from uncomplicated skies.
Water lightly rocks the raft,
laps against the mossy drums.
She is young, lake-slick in her pink suit
with white plastic flowers on the straps.

Outside the rented shoreline cottage
with its oilcloth table and beadboard,
her mother oils and tans, a red scarf
wound gypsy-like in her hair. She hums.
Her other voice, the one honed by litanies
of disappointments, ultimatums,
has not yet reached the horizon.

Her father sits on a campstool in pine shade
wielding his Barlow knife, cleaning and gutting
bluegills, perch, the occasional catfish.
His hands are still deft, sure,
steadily flicking out a shower of scales
like ice chips. There is no tremble.
A cigarette hangs from his lips.

These are the long afternoons,
before the drinking, the leavings,
the cancer. Her sheltering grandparents
doze in the green metal chairs,
her sister and brother dangle
their feet from a dock, stirring
the quick, fingerling minnows.
In that unaware, bright light
of a changeless forever,

all those she loves are safe, good,
they would never hurt her or anyone.
She sees them there, no farther
from a shore she can confidently,
easily reach.

Keegan's Drugstore

Because they knew her there,
my mother cashed a check
where we went for phosphates
and pretzel rods to pay for tickets
on a Greyhound bus to Pittsburgh
where her friend Judy lived.

She left my father a note to find
when he came home to a wife
and the children gone.
She told me these details years later,
that he didn't call once, didn't say
come back, but after a week we did.
There was nowhere else to go.

I remember that store, the counter
with its spinning red and silver stools,
the narrow shelves in the back
lined with cobalt and amber bottles
in their black, steepled tops.
We could get anything there—

caps for cap guns, doll clothes,
model car sets. A white ice chest
sat just inside the door, its heavy lid
releasing a cool fog. She had said,
Wait there, where I longed for
creamsicles, Nutty Buddies, ice cream
with wooden spoons. Soon she
pulled me out to the sidewalk,

into the stifling, summer car,
and an already altered world
where longing and needing would
never be the same thing again,
or so simple, so close.

Appearances

I am eight years old. My mother
and I enter the echoing arcade
of a downtown building
from snow-slick sidewalks
through the fogged, glass blades
of the revolving door I am afraid of,
icy air still knifing my knees.
The passageway glows with
blurry, gauzy clouds I think
must be Christmas lights.

We are coming to pick up
my first pair of glasses,
two tipped, red ovals nested
on green felt lining in a case
that closes with a snap.
Across it, raised gold letters
spell the name of the store
where thin, stacked drawers
pull out like the maps at school.

I am wearing my church gloves
and patent shoes, holding
my mother's hand, my cheek
warm against the dark plush
of her mink coat. Her hat has
a feather and I know she is
beautiful, but she hurries,
so I cannot look up at her
without tripping.

Her heels click and it is cold,
like the time we packed in the night,
and she took us on the train.
I stood on the windy,
steaming platform, the glare

of the station harsh in my eyes.
I didn't know why my father
wasn't with us.

But this is an adventure.
My mother says I will
pay more attention in school,
catch up, not fidget so,
see what I have been missing,
and the haze of problems
the teacher chalks up on
the tilted blackboard—
division, subtraction—
will finally step into their
clear, unmistakable edges.

My Father's Boat

All one winter my father built a boat.
It sat on sawhorses in the garage,
a do-it-yourself, Sunfish dinghy
he bought with cigarette coupons.

Piece by piece he fit together
12 feet of marine plywood on frame
with epoxied puzzle joints that slowly
shaped the broad beam, the V-ed hull
with shallow draft, the dagger board,
an unstayed mast. Done, he painted
a black circle on the lateen sail
and christened it *The Eight Ball.*

The summer before, my parents bought
a vacation home in a raw development
proclaiming its four man-made lakes.
Down oiled gravel roads named
for vanished Indian tribes sat ours—
Eagle Claw—man-made
and small enough to take in
in a glance. My father loved it.

My mother never set foot in the boat,
but my father spent hours on that
murky water with its weedy coves
and sunken trees. One summer
he added oars, another, a trolling motor.
We'd see him out there, just sitting,
sometimes fishing, or trying to catch
any breeze that made it past
that high, earth dam.

But the boat was never practical.
And over time a chronic cough
slowed my father, the lake settled lower
and my mother chafed at the view

disappearing behind the trees and cottages
grown thick around it. When they sold,
The Eight Ball was left decaying
on blocks in the drive, still rigged
with the banner of my father's faded joke.

Visiting Hours with My Grandmother

I am painting her nails when she leans in,
whispers there is a man behind her bed.
Other times he coughs from the curtains.
Bending from her chair to pick
brown leaves from her African violets,
she is careful not to touch him. She *tsks*
when he hitches up his pants in that
nervy way. *Why is he always looking at me,*
she asks, frowning at the drifting drapes
of her *kaltzimmer*. Like a queen, she hands me
a chocolate tin with her favorite opera creams.
The dotted cotton tie-back of her gown
gapes at the neck. Her head, missing
its wig, is a small, hard knoll under wisps
of milkweed silk. She tells me last night
he asked her *Can you explain yourself?*
Do you have any identity? I carefully apply
her red lipstick. She straightens, turns
her cloudy blue eyes to mine, grazing
my cheek with the cool, dry pods of her fingers,
murmuring, *Isn't it strange they let him in?*
My dear, ought I give him a dance?

Mother's Great-Aunt Irene

There were the uncles, of course,
Arvid and Alban, Petersons they were then,
but Oscar, the eldest, born in Sweden,
changed their name to Williams.
He came over with his parents,
Karl and Hedda, to Pierce City, Wisconsin,
then moved over the river to Red Wing,
opened a grocery. We lived above the store,
Mother, and Myrtle and I, just children.
How we loved the ice chips in summer!
And I still can remember the baked apple
I ate on the train I took to see Arvid,
with Myrtle not well and mother poorly
herself by then. They sent me home with
blackberries for her. Can you imagine that,
a small girl, alone on a train?
Then later I married Albert in Wabasha,
had Blaine, fair like all the Williamses.
You should have heard him sing! And hockey,
how he loved it, so quick and graceful,
no one could touch him. I watched him
for hours, cold as it was. When the war came,
he was in college by then, but of course
he had to go. We traveled to Minneapolis
to see him off on the train, so tall
he looked, such a smile, such a kidder.
I was on my way to Hawaii, you know,
when word came he was wounded,
the Pacific. They said he'd get better,
come home, but he never did.
It's so hard, you'll never know.
And my Albert, sick, sick
every day of his life, no help
from that gas, no help at all.
I had to go to work in St. Paul,
signing up recruits.
I play bingo now on Wednesday nights

under their pictures at the VFW.
My beautiful Blainey,
so clever, how he'd tease.
You'll never know.
You go insane.

Photograph of My Father

He reclines in a sunny corner
of the deck in scarf and hat,
despite the mild May day.
He has lost weight from the chemo.
The hat is an old, felt fedora
cocked down at a rakish tilt,
the low brim shadowing his eyes.
He looks like the gambler
he has always been—
craps, blackjack, horses, cards.
He was good at it, playing poker
late into the night with his buddies.
As kids, we'd come down in the morning,
see the eight-sided, green baize table
still up, surrounded by the slag
of ashtrays, half-drained glasses,
the topple of chips he paid us
to sort and box, peeling bills off a roll.
In this picture he looks like a man
about to walk up to a track window,
or lean back in a chair and drag
on a cigarette, calculating
the long shot in his hand.

Too Close to See

for my niece, Jane

When she was nine we were mermaids
bobbing in waves off the Outer Banks,
the soft troughs rhythmically rolling
and lulling us. At night we were
sea lions wallowing in the humid,
teal light of the old, inland motel pool,
fighting off the biting flies. At twelve
she sent me the only other copy
of her handmade book,
so small it fit in my palm,
each page humming with color
and the chrysalis of words.

At sixteen she smiles the smile
of a girl with her braces just off.
Posing by a tree for the yearbook
photographer, she looks as if she is
peering out in a game of hide-and-seek.
Of course she is smiling. Her world
ripens with promise as she climbs into
her friend's car to visit colleges
on the coast, leaving the pattern pieces

of her prom dress laid out
to sew when she returns, leaving
the clutter of makeup, a corkboard
with ticket stubs and photos,
notebooks spilling with poems.
Her parents, as parents do,
have discussed if she could go.
Did one voice caution, the other consent?
Which one urged which?
They would always know.

A truck passed on a hill, or was it
her friend? I refuse to remember
the details. In the story I tell myself,
the photos of the scene show
a girl lying in the grass as if
she is asleep, except for the swan
bend in her neck. In the story
I tell myself, grief will not always
be vast and unanswerable.

Once in Canterbury Cathedral

A small red arrow points "Martyrdom."
It leads to the place where Becket at prayer
bled into the stone at behest of his king.
I silently shuffle past with the rest,
stranger by stranger, over slabs
canted inward by centuries
of pilgrims, petitioners, onlookers.
I am neither saintly or brave, am here only,
some would say, because I am running away.
I even breathe like a runner, sweat in the nights,
feel, as now, walls closing in.
Midway along, the corridor empties
before the first altar. On risers
a clutch of musicians rehearse.
Their delicate, now grandiose strains
splendor up the vast, fanned vault.
We stop, entranced, taking up
our posts as they happen.
Their soloist, the violinist, is Chinese.
It is two days since Tianneman Square.

All these years gone,
still I hear him, see him,
standing forth, eyes closed,
slashing with rapture,
with fury, his impossibly lifting,
insistent crescendo, hauling grace
and grief from the gut
of the strings,
like a child hauled back
by his hair from fire.

At the Other End of the Line

Years ago, my parents called me
from a pay phone at a Kmart
in Michigan City, the night
of my wedding anniversary,
the only ones who remembered.
I relayed weather, news of the boys,
heard them straining to hear
above closing time crowds,
passing the phone between them.
They were on their way home to Ohio
after helping my sister move,
and did I still want that green
cupboard of his mother's?

Hearing their voices, quick, remote,
in the hour of an ordinary evening,
I remember feeling suddenly tender.
They were no longer young,
nor was I, no calendar kept
the days they had wronged me,
as I had wronged them.
We had each outlived ravages
we thought would never be done.
That night the particular story
of hurts did not matter.

I knew I could not imagine
a world where they were not,
where they could not call
or be reached by faulty
but functioning connection,
anchoring the hoardings
and mappings of my life,
to scold, forgive, urge
toward speed limits, sound beds,
safe passage.

Finding My Father

Years after his death, my father came to me
in a dream, walking up from the trim,
grassy slope behind my grandfather's house.
He was smiling, looked rested,
his face and body had fleshed out.
He'd gotten some color back.
He wore a white button-down shirt,
navy blue sweater, tan pants and shoes.
It was close to what he was buried in—
the compromise with my mother as we
picked out the clothes. I wanted
his flannel and denim, she wanted the suit.

In the way of dreams, my father and I
both knew he had died and would die
again in a little while. But first,
we would have time. We would talk.
Sit with the quiet. He would let me
lean against him, curl into his arm,
and when I cried, he wouldn't pull away
or say, "There now, we'll have none of that."

Take Nothing

Not the great blue skimmers warming their wings
in the May sun before flight,
the red-eyed vireos' *here I am, where are you,*
or the radiating catenaries of the weaving spider,
lingering, dew-strung,
not the intricate machinery of the wondrous foot
with one-quarter of the bones in the body,
or the fascicles of nerves firing in the slightest touch,
not the easy assumption of motion
in neck, limbs, torso,
not the syrupy evening light of summer,
somewhere bees gravid with pollen
and the promise of rain, not August's crickets
whirring their incessant clockwork,
not the white-bearded waves following in furrows,
the boom and bravura of surf,
or its lace and small applause,
not the guttural rubato in the throat
at the end of the barn owl's call,
or the orange Chinese lanterns of persimmons,
not the way the light bends in autumn's russet afternoons,
or the fraying draperies of fog in the hollows,
not the faithful bellows of the lungs,
the free-flowing tributaries of the heart,
or the black, rickety branches of trees against
a full winter moon, like the raised hands
of Giotto's saints in prayer,
not the tellers of night tales,
or the light from extinguished stars,
not the friable fabric of memory,
nor any love's precarious survival,
not even the soul at night—
take nothing,
nothing for granted.
Not in this world.

Waiting for the Perseid Meteor Shower

A dogtooth moon, horned and dim,
hangs over the suck of midnight tide,
the skirt of beach, where wet gusts spin
the wind socks, flog the docks of cottages.

We are silent except for the ice
in our glasses, the creak of rockers,
eyes raised to the ruined
theater of stars.

We have come here
to the continent's edge,
like plunderers, to see what
can be salvaged from the wreckage

we have made. Here is a spar
of pain, is that some rigging
of hope? I don't even know
what we are looking for—

stars flashing from black curtains,
some fire-fall of legend,
red snakes in the sky,
a revelation so obvious

they say the casual eye
can't mistake it. Wordless,
we wait for signs, earthy
or celestial, something more

than the remote Morse of a plane,
a whittled moon and the wheel
of Orion into the sea.
The August night steams on,

yields nothing to the watch
we keep. What's become
of all the storied gold
our nights once showered down?

Is there nothing left within us
to pick the lock of dark?

Parallax

*parallax: the different appearances of an object
depending on the angle of observation*

Tonight on Kitt Peak, Atacama,
Mauna Kea, the vast wheels
of lenses curved to the sky
see nothing we see,
our connected dots of queens
and heroes shape cartoons
as should shame us.
Yet even the sublime complexity
of our galactic emissaries
pings back tales as primitive.

Their quests have incised my lifeline.
Voyagers set forth when I was young,
Magellan sailed through a year of passings.
My sons grew tall through Galileo,
its instruments primed to find
a pulse no stronger than a common
porch light, as its merest filaments
swept the great simoons of Mars,
the scored mirror of Europa,
the stone face of Ganymede.

Life bends like light to its opposite.
All the dark tells is already the past.
Even in the foreknown wake
of mere prodigal comets,
when the next returns
the youngest among us
will be old, the old gone
to dust. Who might even
be here to know a sign,
a signal, eons after it uttered?

Probe as we will by eye, seer
or aperture, we still insist on
the shadowy caves and fissures
of human scale and time,
where wavering candles bracket
the brief flare of our lives,
fabling the dark,
not with pulsars and quasars,
but with our own imprints
and reflections in lyre and eagle,
archer and swan.

White Cyclamens

Like the underskin of an onion,
this February sky stretches thin,
opaque, greasy with four days' rain.
There is nothing not sodden with it—
the boggy lawn, cold-running gulleys,
cascading eaves. How can there be
so much of one thing, given so
prodigally? Such openness scares me,
who gives in such careful measure,
when needed, when asked.
I would never waste myself like that.
So I set by my desk white cyclamens
with their silky, pristine petals,
like formal white-gloved palms
drawing politely back, or tucked
like fine handkerchiefs
in the precise, green pocket of leaves.

On Old State Route 10

The van passed me
doing 70
80 maybe
ahead clear
county road
and the dog
bucking out
from a drive
a gravel drive
on the right
big   brown
head like a bear
black muzzle
racing at
the road
I saw
didn't see
I saw it hit
turning under
the van
the axle
like brushes
in a car wash
it hit
rolled
hit   a sack
a burlap sack
spilled   trying
to rise
I swung tight
radio on
windows up
heard   sounds
a part of
me slipping
out the windshield
saying   I'm leaving

you are going
to have
an accident.

Contingencies

The rat snake,
five feet and black as shredded tire,
tracked a languid *s* across the drive,
heading for the duff along the fence.
I could have killed it with the car
or ungated the dogs, but gave it
my small god reprieve.

Later I found
its thick, black coil at the base
of the children's old basketball stand,
the head just swaying out from the body.
Its milky underbelly keeled and wrapped
like a strap around the pole.
It started to climb.

Then I saw the nest,
tucked in an angle bracket twelve feet up
behind the backboard, a furtive pocket
of leaves and twigs, a sprig of moss,
the work of a wren, those agile,
spring darters who built anywhere
that stood still long enough.

It must have seemed
safe that high. I felt the recoil through my body,
watching as the looped bulk
now bunched at the back
of the rusted hoop,
its tail tapering down,
a cipher of the precarious.

Argentine Tango Flash Mob, Budapest

In the mid-town West End Mall,
amid evening crowds strolling the bright-lit,
indoor boulevards offering Nikes, Xboxes,
and banks, luxury perfumes, leather goods,
Gap and confectioners with marzipan,
amid the people mingling in food courts,
idly conversing over nyagi pancakes, pizza
and McDonald's, under the exotic palms
in the high, wide atrium, where myriad lights
float in a dark pool and a lanky man
in sneakers and blue cardigan talks
on his phone, a woman sits on a low stage

and stretches the accordion folds of a long,
black box. Then pressing the small keys,
she begins to make the minor chords of
an ineffable yearning sing on the *bandeleon*.
Another joins in, then a third with a small guitar,
their music rising and inviting until
the man in the cardigan gathers himself,
then precisely embraces air. *Abrazo*.

He steps back—*atrás*, to the side—*al castado*,
then forward, gives a small swivel
with his hips. Ten feet behind him,
a woman in pink jeans steps toward him
in her own *caminada*. A couple emerges
from the crowd, a woman's arm reaching
along the shoulder of her partner,
her hand near his neck—*apilado*.

A barrista in a red apron leaves her cafe,
a man leaves the Kitty Watch kiosk,
sheds his parka, and there are four,
then ten, twenty couples materialize.

They are torso to torso, heartbeat
to heartbeat. Then fifty are moving,
turning, points in a slowly spiraling
galaxy of lovers, strangers, friends,
bystanders beguiled from Vodaphone,
a Football Fan Store, the lottery shop,
some dancing *con cruzada*,
then reversing—*ocho adelanta*—
others moving in *ocho basico*,
hesitant, smiling, improvising,

each mirroring each, in this improbable
no-time, without urgency or purpose,
no before or after, where there is only
this other and their embrace—breath
and answer—before the music is over
and they discover they are already late
and hurry away into a night in which
they will later find themselves
strangely humming, longing.

In the Waiting Area

Outside, the abrupt, keening chaos
of an ambulance broke over
the morning streets, its startled cadence
of calamity coming through
the buffering trees into the hush
of a doctor's waiting room.

Inside, the sounds were wind flutes,
water, strings. I thought of a glass
harmonica, its myriad globes
like the jars that once drew out fevers,
just as this music was meant to
draw out all that was noisome inside.

We were so quiet. Only the antiphonal
flick of magazines played irregularly
above it. On the hour, the doctor would
talk in syllables cushioned like this room—
tapping, tapping, like a spoon
around an egg.

It was that kind of waiting,
that kind of doctor. No siren for
the jarring box of the mind.
And you were waiting, too,
wishing there were racing engines,
some wild alarm, a saving grace

you could lift and carry me toward.

Chance

       The dream of dreams—
to unwind time,
to set another course,
give another answer.
It is the haunter of crossroads
and high places, the familiar
of winter dusk, the shadow
at the edge of sleep,
scraps to the dogs
of wakefulness—
to have the chance to do it over,
get it right this time, the choice
you would not make again,
the risk you would not fail.

       And in that past
you would give anything to enter,
has everything stood still,
remained, by ingenious
suspension, untouched,
intact as in a snow globe?
Shake it.
What swirls about?
In that blur, can you precisely
say, *here it was, here*
the coordinates were set,
the decision gone
beyond reversing?
Was it so clear?
Was it really all you?
Don't bet your life on it.

The Healer

She lays her palms on the crown of my head
as if she is calling up strength to enter
the waste of nettles and steeps that live
in my stony skin. When she traces
its gradient, I think she can read all
that has hardened there. My spine
is a sunken tree trunk the unwary
wreck on, my shoulders a wedge of clay.
I have given myself up to this rudiment touch,
as her fingers press weighted and sure
as the bent necks of shorebirds.
A scent of geraniums follows her wrists.
I want to lift out of this body,
ragged, beset. I want to grow wings.
She probes along the ribs, blades,
as slowly I begin to feel loosed, new,
not wings, but something to hold,
a beginning, like a cradle
rocking in her hands,
a small boat set forth upon water.

Voyage Out

A small rain rattles in the leaves,
moonlight pillowcases the porch.
Our son moves off through the woods,
a fitful, brooding glow
from the flashlight in his hand.
You pace in your thoughts,
as far away as if we knew
no language between us.

How charged the night air is,
ripe and restless.
We all move separately, expectantly,
how strong the urge to decision,
as we wait for weather or circumstance
to compel us, as if we are poised
at the start of an unknown journey
over the chartless water.

I see it comes simply to this—
what are we willing to risk,
into what silence
are we ready to speak?
No story tells ours.
The shadows on our faces come
from rooms that are behind us.
The wind is a rope paying out.
Alone or together,
our running lights
are in our eyes.

Wing and a Prayer

Make me an angel with a gypsy heart,
find me a place in that angel band.
Give me a honey and steel soprano,
a rodeo skirt and a guitar that strums
from blue ridge to badlands to badass
and back through the hardscrabble hollows.
Make me the rambling kind, a scuffed-boots
girl on a red dirt road, the diamond
in a coal dust town. I'd be Sweet Annie,
Evangeline, songbird of branch creeks,
fading trains and prairies with a
silver-dollar moon. I'd sing those crystal
harmonies, so aching and sweet,
of highways and heartbreaks sighing
in a cottonwood wind. I'd be the long,
high lonesome, the lowdown
and down so low, the soft heart
and the hard row.
One of these days I'll ride a river
until the tide runs out,
I'll waltz across Texas,
I'll be the dancer
in those golden slippers
lifted into grace.

In My Next Life

I am born in Wyoming, in the foothills
of the Casper Mountains where the mist
rises thick from the North Platte River.
Our ranch raises Paso Finos, Columbus'
lost horses of "the beautiful step."
The Cheyenne in my blood shows in
my cheekbones and I know the name
of every tree on the slopes, every flower
in the fields and can read the winds
of weather as if they are script in the sky.
When the lie-down heat of summer comes,
or winter ice skitters the horses,
my father schools me in classics,
history and languages. My mother
teaches me art, music, the arcana
of herbs and a weakness for old stock
roses—the rugosas, centifolias,
albas and the damascenes
brought back by Crusaders from
the Citadel gates of Saladin.

I will travel, wrap in saris of Rajasthani
silk, ride the plains of Andalusia,
wear amber amulets from the Caucasus,
wake to the echo of goat bells on Mykonos.
But home will remain these hills,
the timbered, wide-windowed house,
the doorway still redolent with roses,
where books and photographs stack
on the burled desk my father built
and Majolica and Ming from my mother
mingle anyhow on the sunlit kitchen table.

If I have regrets, they will be no more
than the ordinary ones—a wish
that languished, chances missed,
a love that lasted past its time

and one not long enough.
I will know that time neither hastens
or lingers. It is simply itself
and life the residue of attention
we bring to its moments. I will know
it is the gift that must be opened,
before it passes like shadows
over the mountains.

At the Next Congregation
for the Causes of Saints

There are seven saints for brides, four for marital woes,
five for infidelity, in addition to the assemblage for divorce,
difficult in-laws and troublesome servants. Brewers, bees
and lace makers have four apiece, while two saints extend
patronage to hair stylists, another intercedes for the circus.
The patron of dogs is distinct from that for dog fanciers.
Fully covered are flight attendants, Alpine guides and gondoliers,
toy makers, poultry, pickpockets and pastry chefs, glovers,
lawyers, hardware and hosiery, as well as that vast
compendia of ailments poor flesh is heir to, not omitting
sleepwalking, apoplexy, hangovers, possession and piles.

At the next Congregation for the Causes of Saints, I say
let there also be saints for the passed over, the negligible,
the left behind and left out. For snails, grocery baggers,
museum guards, and benches in snow. Let there be a saint
for awkward children, the shy, the uncertain, too large
or too small in their bodies, holders of books and hiders
in trees. Call their saint Secretus the Younger. And while
there is already a saint for disappointing children,
where is the saint for disappointing parents? May
new-minted Perseverian be elevated into the fold.

Let there also be a saint for attic chairs with their broken
wicker seats that once rocked infants, for unwound
pocket watches and bowls of aging potpourri. Let her name
be Dustinia. For the verified miracles of the open place,
the sympathetic trooper, the canceled meeting, the snowy day,
give gratitude to overlooked St. Breezius. May further prayers
be raised to Chordius, saint for unwanted bookcase pianos
that they be brought to children playing "Heart and Soul"
in camp halls and "Chopsticks" in bible school basements.

And for weeds, with no one to advocate their cause,
though three saints hold a celestial place for florists,
I propose someone humble, unstinting—say, St. Diminimus—
intercessory for purslane in lawns, the great mulleins
and burdocks of the fields, sharp teasels and scorch-topped
cat-tails in gulley-swamps, hardy fleabane and Scotch broom
braving the broken roadsides, all necessary to some
living thing, however small it may be, that like saints
and their blessings sometimes go unseen and unrecognized.

Encounter

Coming from the car, I saw
a large, red-tailed hawk,
talons gripping the arm
of the plaid lawn chair
no more than twenty feet away.
It did not startle, shift—
just cocked the copper curve
of its head, sharpening
the profile of the black, sickle beak,
the thick, mottled plumage
across the breadth of its chest.

It seemed waiting.
For a quivering vole gone to ground?
A rabbit reckless with inattention?
Even me? Not prey,
but a challenge? a charge?
Someone to witness. Marvel.
Acknowledge. To be—
there's no other word for it—
enraptured.

We stayed like that.
Then nonchalantly it rose
on its four-foot wingspan
in low, easy strokes
over the lawn, lifting
and topping the pine crowns,
until it was a dark crossbow,
far and slant, circling
impossibly high in the blank blue.
All right, I thought. You win.

Snapping Turtle

I knew at once what it was,
stopped in the middle of the road,
though I'd never seen one—
the large, elongated platter,
almost flat, black as if with tarnish.

What had brought it into the open,
made it climb from the sinking muck
of a creek somewhere, up through
thickets of briars and sedge?

I pulled over, meaning to coax it across
before another car came over the rise.
Sticky summer heat simmered up
from the pavement as I crouched
and crooked my fingers.

The hooded head came part way out
from layers of scaly folds. Its blunt
snout lifted, scenting, the long neck
like a blind snake emerging from
a subterranean cave.

I clicked at it. Its black, aqueous eyes
swiveled and fixed on me.
The lids gave one deliberate blink.
Then the raptor-like mouth opened
and thick, powerful legs
suddenly pushed it forward.

I looked into something primeval,
remnant of an ancient, unfathomable age,
millions of years' survival in
the concentrated menace of its advance.

Then someone was coming.
A man in a pickup slowed,
halted at low idle, watching.
I smelled exhaust, tar and swamp.
Then he shifted and pulled past,
his head leaning out the window
calling, "Damn fool,
those'll take your arm off
in a second."

Currents

In the steep, curving gorge of Nantahala,
about a mile below Santeelah Dam,
the Cheoha River gains speed on a rare
straightaway, hurtling over a warren
of rocks and rubble. Granite slabs rise
as if breaching, rapids smacking in a boil
of foam and funnels and the crests
of a thousand small falls spangle in
the sun like crushed green foil.

There, in a place where silt and driftwood
make a narrow strip for rushes and scrub,
I saw a great blue heron. It stood in
magnificent stillness, with the rash din
of the river sounding ceaselessly past.
Its body was the gray of the underside
of clouds, of fogs rising in forest coves
before morning burns them away.

Then it took a delicate, stately step
on impossibly thin legs,
hinged like ribs of a folding umbrella.
Resettling, it arched its wings, brushed
with the blue of the washed sky
on certain rare days over the ocean.
The heron was in no hurry. It stood
in an effortless balance between chaos
and calm. I could not watch it in a hurry.
I could not watch it with any sense of

time passing, or even waiting,
for waiting means time. For a moment,
I turned, but looking back I could not
find it again. It had disappeared,
camouflaged against the gray green
of the bank, or gone on its half glide,
half flight farther along the Cheoah,

swelled by the Yellow Hammer
and Sweetwater creeks, surging in turn
toward the Little Tennessee.
So moments flow.
Then time stirred, and I knew
that a curtain I had not been aware
was there had lifted, parted, closed.

Gold Triumph Tulips

*A chair is a difficult object. A skyscraper is
almost easier.*
　　　　　—Mies van der Rohe

The stems strict as a regiment,
the perfectly balanced bell,
the saturated yellow primary as a crayon,
angled petals smooth as thumbed wax,
slightly reflexed along the crest,
poised to glide, plane from plane,
into a goblet of light. Pure Bauhaus.
Nothing here of the *passementerie*
of fringe tulips, the gaudy streaks
and graffiti of the parrots,
the voluptuaries of tulip peonies.
Such clarity, stricture, dominion.
Van der Rohe himself
might almost have signed them.

In the Poetry Workshop

I cannot tell them how it is,
the trap some inexplicably
fall into, this tangle with words,
while others step safely around it.
They bring me the broken
pieces of their lives—
their mother's vacant nights,
a brother's cries, hands washed
thirty times a day—betrayals,
needs, loves laid in my lap
like so many broken springs,
bits of brass, the odd
bent cog, and I,
small god, watchmaker,
moony eye in place
will see what they cannot,
decode what they won't say,
give the coil a knock, a whirr,
set it all to rights.
They are angry when it doesn't tick.
They are sure there is something
I am holding back.
How do I tell them
all poets' hands are empty?
On the hour, they file out,
skeptics at the mystery.
All I know is somehow,
suddenly, it will happen
and the words will be there,
where they always were,
in the voice between
two silences.

The Philosopher in the Mountains

Last night the early star.
Then ghost trails obscuring
the moon. Now my feet bare
in the beads of rain the morning
has left on the stone flagging
of the walk. Great, gray clouds
hang like sacks that may
or may not spill again, sinking
to meet the drifts of mist
from the valley. A dark bird banks,
enters them. Impassable
the mud-slick paths to the top.
Portents? Is it too late?

*

So infatuated once with mind.
Finding a way through labyrinths
of words. Breaking and breaking down
the questions, tilting at subtleties,
the gleam of a system, the lure
of something incontrovertible,
so indelible as to be impervious
to subsequent correction.
The thing itself. Radical essence.
The one irreducible stone
at the bottom of the well.
A stone to begin.
Then another to balance.
The seed and the split seed rooting.

*

Still the old bafflements—
to reach beyond assumption.
The inescapability of performance.
What was the point, after all?

The thing or the inference?
Or the no-thing beyond it?
Or simply to know how to go
unaccompanied to our end?

★

A closed book. I am done
with distant reports.
So much I cannot recall.
But this morning I notice everything.
This present. The leap and rush
the rains have brought
to a nearby rill. A sound
in the leaves like the rustle
of skirts. The brimming bowl
set out for the hidden bird
whose gliding notes I hear.
Something small I should
have learned, like the harvester
of tea leaves, the artisan
of this perfect cup, warm
and gold in my palm.
Unbidden the memory
of a quick, light step,
the midnight of her hair.

Landfall

Once, driving home for a visit, we left
Carolina in the dark, the children slipping
back to dreams we'd roused them from.
At last the remnant moon leached into
dawn as we crossed the second state line
and yolky light revealed a passing
landscape of canted warehouses, car lots,
scrapyards and abandoned factories
looking like the insides of old radios.
Then morning rose up like a window shade.

We, too, came slowly into the day,
the children reassuming their shapes
from the heap of slumped coats. Traffic
swelled by the hour, cars funneling down
from the on-ramps, RVs lumbering
up the grades, long hauls playing tag,
and a trooper leisurely backing up lines
as he flirted with a girl at the tollbooth.
Hours streamed by in a rhythmic daze
of desultory talk, music, the backseat chirps
of games. By midafternoon, we finally

left the interstate for two-lane roads,
rattling past corncribs, grain elevators,
the autumn finished fields of the fertile,
combed floodplains of southern Ohio,
when it came without warning—
inexplicable, something I was fearful,
almost ashamed, to name, there
and then gone, something pure—
like peace—as our fragile world

crossed over the blue,
cantilevered bridge
flinging its steel cat's cradle

across the great moving river.

A Moment

My sons, four and seven, in yellow slickers,
were coming down the long, gravel drive
in the rain, carrying the morning paper.
Their black umbrellas crazily swayed
and jaunted above them. I could see only
their legs until they tilted their awkward
awnings back like the Morton Salt girl.
Their joy brimmed over every puddle,
every emphatic stomp of their soaked-through
shoes. They paused, waved to where
I stood at the kitchen window,
in the ache of that ancient longing—
a child's approach, return.

Late August

The lavender rinse of early sky is slowly
going to gold. From near trees come
the low notes of a mourning dove like breath
blowing over a bottle, the rusty bicker
of a jay. Neither the hummingbird
in the flame-heads of lantana or bees
deep in the scarlet mallow have left
for the winter that still seems distant.

This is the ripe hour—this balanced
tip of time, when light warms
the dew-damp grass, an hour when
the body feels strangely loosed
into spirit and spirit loosed into world.
I feel it hover here in the drowse
of summer's ending, before the kindled
forfeits of fall, the sharp and glittery
clarities that follow,
an hour asking its question
of what to yield to, and when.

Canto

For spirit, I give you the heron lifting in flexed elegance
from the gray-blanched sycamores of the marsh.

For promise, I give you the mossy overhang of April bluets,
yellow violets with their brook trout leaves,
and tadpoles still a nova of apple seeds.

For moodiness, I give you the raked clouds of the mackerel sky,
the restless arcs in the topmost sway of the pines.

For trust, I give you my body, a raft in the currents of sleep.
I give you desire still desiring, the pleasure-taking eye.

For grief, I give you the muscular, granite-grained ironwoods,
the fraught branches of the ice storm and the risk that comes of it.

For time to come, I give you the horned owl that waits as it will
in the dogwood at dusk, its great head supple as a temple dancer's.

For time that is, I give you the February cardinal on the rain-black branch,
that small, fierce, blood-colored flag of life.

The Dream of Eadfrith

Early in the 8th century, the Lindisfarne Gospels,
a masterpiece of manuscript color and design, was
produced on Holy Island, Northumbria. The entire
work was done by one monk, Eadfrith.

I

According to the writings of Benedict
and Cassiodorus, who rule such things,
I have been given extra candles, a sundial
for the passage of day, a water clock
for the hours of night. Beside me sits
the codex of St. Jerome to copy.
For my work the skins of a hundred calves
have been brined, boiled, stretched
and stretched again to a fine thinness,
pegs ever turning on the tightening rack,
then scraped with the curved lunellum
lest a knife pierce them, then pumiced
and pressed with white powder, until cut
and folded to pages of smoothest vellum.
Ink from lampblack and glair awaits my quill,
my pigments await my brush.

II

The air is so cold it seems it must shatter.
The chill-blue hour of early stars now shows
above the horizon. It is the gray blue of herons
in the marshes. Soon night will be black as
cormorants' wings with their iridescent sheen.
Rime frost rims the island's outcrops,
the coastal cliffs where colonies of graylags
and storm petrels have their season's roost.
Gone are the curlews and terns weaving
over the broad shingles and tidal flats.
Gone, too, the sparrow hawks, plovers and kestrels

I was accustomed to watch on sunstruck,
midsummer days. How I would lose myself
in their loops and arcs—a glory of wings.

III

As the hours shorten, so does my own light.
How many winters are left ahead? Only Heaven
takes no heed of time, like the sea that washes
up the beach, leaves, then washes back again.
Tonight its surface is like shaken silk, the soft silver
of the breast of guillemots and the wings
of kittiwakes. To capture such colors, I have
gathered materials from the fields, woodlands
and shore, working them with mortar and pestle
and in the grinding stones of my quern.
For blues, I have woad, the Asp of Jerusalem,
cut only from the first year's stalks and leaves,
mashed, fermented and dried. Under my hand
it will give back the changing lapis and indigos
of the tides, the sky-blue of forget-me-nots,
the violet-tinge in eye-bright, the purple
throat of the marsh orchid.

Weld, that they call Dyer's Weed, yields
its brilliant lemons and yellows if harvested
in high summer when its sinuous stems
still carry their flowers. To these belong
the yellow of stonecrop, the glow of bog flag,
and waxy, flaxen saxifrage. For green,
I have flaked verdigris from copper
soaked in vinegar. For reds, I have minium
from white lead tempered in the fire—
for the crimson of field garlic and ripe ripples
of rowan fruit and haw-berries. With chalk
and bone ash, it gives the pink of sea thrift,
the shades of centaury and rockrose—

also the russet of the red squirrel, the fox,
the roe deer, and breast of the godwit,
the tawny cat and the rabbit it watches.

IV

Do I dream here in the dark?
Has some power thus ensnared me
unawares, attached me too much
to this world? Is it vanity to wish
to leave some trace of myself,
of this riot and density of invention?
Sometimes I feel I could ask for nothing
more than to come upon the world
made new after the shiver and stir of rain—
to see the pale, green-golds in the spring fringes
of catkins swaying from oak and hornbeam,
the rich plush of moss, the silvered lichen,
the marram grass stitching the dunes,
the cloud-wet woods, the purpled whorls
of shells, and the chevron of birds
descending, ascending.

2003
Trouble, Mary Baine Campbell
A Place Made of Starlight, Peter Cooley
Taking Down the Angel, Jeff Friedman
Lives of Water, John Hoppenthaler
Imitation of Life, Allison Joseph
Except for One Obscene Brushstroke, Dzvinia Orlowsky
The Mastery Impulse, Ricardo Pau-Llosa
Casino of the Sun, Jerry Williams

2004
The Women Who Loved Elvis All Their Lives, Fleda Brown
The Chronic Liar Buys a Canary, Elizabeth Edwards
Freeways and Aqueducts, James Harms
Prague Winter, Richard Katrovas
Trains in Winter, Jay Meek
Tristimania, Mary Ruefle
Venus Examines Her Breast, Maureen Seaton
Various Orbits, Thom Ward

2005
Things I Can't Tell You, Michael Dennis Browne
Bent to the Earth, Blas Manuel De Luna
Blindsight, Carol Hamilton
Fallen from a Chariot, Kevin Prufer
Needlegrass, Dennis Sampson
Laws of My Nature, Margot Schilpp
Sleeping Woman, Herbert Scott
Renovation, Jeffrey Thomson

2006
Burn the Field, Amy Beeder
The Sadness of Others, Hayan Charara
A Grammar to Waking, Nancy Eimers
Dog Star Delicatessen: New and Selected Poems 1979–2006,
    Mekeel McBride
Shinemaster, Michael McFee

Selected Early Poems: 1958-1983, Greg Kuzma
The Other Life: Selected Poems, Herbert Scott
Admission, Jerry Williams

2011
Having a Little Talk with Capital P Poetry, Jim Daniels
Oz, Nancy Eimers
Working in Flour, Jeff Friedman
Scorpio Rising: Selected Poems, Richard Katrovas
The Politics, Benjamin Paloff
Copperhead, Rachel Richardson

2012
Now Make an Altar, Amy Beeder
Still Some Cake, James Cummins
Comet Scar, James Harms
Early Creatures, Native Gods, K. A. Hays
That Was Oasis, Michael McFee
Blue Rust, Joseph Millar
Spitshine, Anne Marie Rooney
Civil Twilight, Margot Schilpp

2013
Oregon, Henry Carlile
Selvage, Donna Johnson
At the Autopsy of Vaslav Nijinksy, Bridget Lowe
Silvertone, Dzvinia Orlowsky
Fibonacci Batman: New & Selected Poems (1991-2011), Maureen Seaton
When We Were Cherished, Eve Shelnutt
The Fortunate Era, Arthur Smith
Birds of the Air, David Yezzi

2014
Night Bus to the Afterlife, Peter Cooley
Alexandria, Jasmine Bailey
Dear Gravity, Gregory Djanikian
Pretenders, Jeff Friedman

2018
World Without Finishing, Peter Cooley
May Is an Island, Jonathan Johnson
The End of Spectacle, Virginia Konchan
Big Windows, Lauren Moseley
Bad Harvest, Dzvinia Orlowsky
The Turning, Ricardo Pau-Llosa
Immortal Village, Kathryn Rhett
No Beautiful, Anne Marie Rooney
Last City, Brian Sneeden
Imaginal Marriage, Eleanor Stanford
Black Sea, David Yezzi

2019
The Complaints, W. S. Di Piero
Brightword, Kimberly Burwick
Ordinary Chaos, Kimberly Kruge
Mad Tiny, Emily Pettit
Afterswarm, Margot Schilpp

2020
Sojourners of the In-Between, Gregory Djanikian
Any God Will Do, Virginia Konchan
My Second Work, Bridget Lowe
Flourish, Dora Malech
Take Nothing, Deborah Pope